MATT CHRISTOPHER

On the Bike with...

Lance Armstrong

MATT CHRISTOPHER

On the Bike with...

Text by Glenn Stout

 LITTLE, BROWN AND COMPANY

New York ∗ Boston

Little, Brown and Company

Time Warner Book Group
1271 Avenue of the Americas, New York, NY 10020
Visit our Web site at www.lb-kids.com

www.mattchristopher.com

First Revised Edition: 2005

Matt Christopher® is a registered trademark of
Matt Christopher Royalties, Inc.

Cover photograph by Stringer Rothermel

Library of Congress Cataloging-in-Publication Data

Christopher, Matt.
   On the bike with — Lance Armstrong / Matt Christopher — 1st ed.
      p. cm.
   Summary: A biography of the enthusiastic cyclist whose racing career
was interrupted by a battle with cancer before getting back on track
with a Tour de France win.
   ISBN 0-316-07549-3 (pb)
   1. Armstrong, Lance — Juvenile literature.   2. Cyclists — United
States — Biography — Juvenile literature.   3. Cancer — Patients —
United States — Biography — Juvenile literature.   [1. Armstrong,
Lance.   2. Bicyclists.   3. Cancer — Patients.]   I. Title: Lance Arm-
strong.   II. Title.

GV1051.C76 C47 2003
796.6'2'092 — dc21
[B]   2002022490

10 9 8 7 6 5 4 3 2

COM-MO

Printed in the United States of America

Contents

Chapter One:
1971–1983

A Boy and His Bike

Most kids love riding bicycles. Whether it's riding a bike to school, visiting friends, or just taking a trip to the library, riding a bike is a great way to get around and get some exercise. Sometimes it's even fun just to start riding and enjoy the journey without knowing where you'll end up.

When he was a boy, Lance Armstrong loved riding his bike. Riding allowed him to go places he couldn't have gone otherwise and helped him forget his troubles. Since his childhood, riding a bike has taken him places he couldn't have imagined — bike racing, or cycling, has taken Armstrong around the world and made him the greatest bike racer of his time. Armstrong has been a world champion, an Olympian, and a three-time winner of the Tour de France, the ultimate bicycle race.

But even more important, cycling has helped make Lance Armstrong the person he is today. While growing up, Lance felt isolated and was unhappy. He didn't get along with his stepfather and didn't know what he was going to do with his life.

Cycling changed his life and changed him. His success as a cyclist has given Armstrong confidence and strength, helping him survive his battle with cancer. Many athletes might have retired from their sport after such an experience, but Armstrong came back stronger than ever before. His life has been an inspiration to others who have faced serious illness.

During his childhood in the small Texas town of Plano, Lance admits, "I never dreamed about winning the Tour de France as a kid." In fact, he never dreamed of becoming a cyclist. Like many Americans, he didn't even know that bike racing was a sport.

While cycling has always been very popular in Europe, when Lance was a boy the sport was almost unknown in the United States. Most people thought riding bikes was just for kids.

The bike was invented in the late 1700s, and as the design of bicycles improved and the manufacturing process made them more widely available, the sport of cycling evolved. The first races took place in the 1860s. Competitors raced one another over long distances on highways. Spectators would line the roads to watch the cyclists whiz past them. Other kinds of races, such as hill climbs, time trials, and races against the clock over measured distances, were also popular.

In the late 1800s and early 1900s, the greatest cyclist in the world was a man named Marshall W. "Major" Taylor. Major Taylor was an African American, and throughout his career in cycling, he faced racism and prejudice. But his determination helped him break through color barriers to become a world champion.

At the beginning of the twentieth century, race organizers tried to make the races more exciting for fans. They built banked, oval-shaped indoor tracks called velodromes. Fans were able to see the entire race while sitting in chairs around the outside of the track.

The building of velodromes inspired different kinds of races. In addition to time trials, sprints, and long-distance races, cyclists also competed in cycling marathons that lasted for days. Some races lasted nearly a week!

By the 1930s, cycling had lost its popularity. Other sports, such as football and basketball, boomed, while competitive cycling almost died out in the United States. But in Europe cycling remained popular. Road racing, in particular, captured the imaginations of fans and competitors.

Most major road races take place over a number of days; each day, cyclists participate in a different stage of the race. They race against one another, and officials keep track of how fast each rider completes each stage. The overall winner is the rider who completes all the stages in the least amount of time. Winning an entire race takes talent, stamina, and strategy.

While the cyclists race against one another, they also race as part of a team. Each team of six to eight cyclists works to help one member of the team, the leader, win. They do this by setting the pace and by helping to protect the leader from the wind, and taking turns riding just in front of him to keep him strong.

But sometimes the leader will charge ahead of everyone to win a stage. This is called a breakaway and usually happens near the end of a race.

4

The most famous race in the world, the Tour de France, first took place in 1903. The race takes several weeks to complete and is made up of more than twenty stages, covering a total of more than two thousand miles. The cyclists race on roads throughout France, which are closed to cars during each stage. Some stages are short sprints, others are races nearly two hundred miles long on relatively flat terrain, and still others wind through mountains. Some stages take eight hours or more to complete.

In order to win the Tour de France, a cyclist must be able to ride fast on the flat stages and have the strength to climb the hills. The cyclist must also have enough stamina to race six to eight hours a day for several weeks. Fans line the course, and a huge crowd usually forms near the end of the race. The winner of the Tour de France is considered the greatest cyclist in the world and becomes an international celebrity. In Europe, children dream of winning the Tour de France just as American children dream of winning an Olympic gold medal.

But when Lance Armstrong was a child, he didn't know anything about the Tour de France. Winning the Tour de France was about as likely a thing for

Lance to do as walking on the moon. As Lance later described his upbringing, "We were middle-class at best. You don't always have the capacity for big dreams — you don't even know what to dream." He had a lot of obstacles to overcome.

Lance was born on September 18, 1971. His mother, Linda, had married young. She was only seventeen years old and had to drop out of high school when she became pregnant with Lance. Lance's father wasn't much older; the young couple divorced when Lance was still a baby.

Lance's mother was determined to be the best mother she could be. "I wanted him to be special," she later recalled. She leaned on her parents and family for support. They didn't have much money but helped her as much as they could. Still, Linda knew that it was up to her to make a life for her son. "For a long time there was just the two of us," Linda later explained. "All I did, my life, was going to work and raising my son, and I was happy to do it."

She moved with Lance into a small apartment in a suburb of Dallas, Texas. She worked hard and often had more than one job, working at a fast-food restaurant, a grocery store, and an office to earn enough money for rent, food, and day care for her young son. At the same time, she went back to school to earn her high school diploma so she and Lance could have a better life.

Despite her busy schedule, she spent as much time as she possibly could with Lance. Even though she would be tired at the end of the day, she always made time to play with him, read to him, and give him the love and care he needed.

After she graduated, Linda got a better job as a secretary and moved with Lance to another Dallas suburb, Richardson. She also married a man named Terry Armstrong, who adopted Lance. The young family was better off than before.

Once a week, Lance's mother would take him to a doughnut shop near their apartment to have a treat for breakfast. On the way to the doughnut shop was a neighborhood bike shop. Each week when Lance and his mother would walk by the bike shop, Lance would look longingly at the bicycles in the window and parked on the sidewalk.

Although he never asked his mother to buy him a bike, she could tell he wanted one, but she couldn't afford it. The man who owned the store, Jim Hoyt, would occasionally step outside and chat with the young mother and her son.

He could tell that Lance wanted a bike, too, but from talking to Lance's mother, he knew the young family didn't have much money. One day, he offered Linda a deal on a small brown bike with yellow wheels. She knew Lance would enjoy it. A lot of young boys and girls in Lance's neighborhood already had bikes, and she didn't want her son to feel left out. He'd already learned to ride by borrowing bikes from his friends. She could afford the bike at the price Hoyt offered and bought it for Lance.

Lance loved his bike. His stepfather was very strict, and when they argued, Lance would jump on his bike and ride away with his friends. The roads in and around Richardson were flat and straight, and Lance would ride for hours.

He didn't realize it, but with each stroke of the pedals he was on his way to becoming a cyclist. The roads from Richardson would eventually take him around the world.

Chapter Two:
1983-1986

The Iron Kid

When Lance was about twelve years old, the Armstrongs bought a house and moved to the nearby city of Plano. Lance tried hard to make new friends and fit into his neighborhood, but he felt awkward and alone. Plano was a much wealthier community than Richardson; they'd been able to afford the house there because of Linda's success at her job. Lance realized it was a step up for the family, but he sensed that some of the other kids looked down on him.

Most of the popular boys in town played sports. Football and baseball were the biggest sports in Plano, particularly football. The high school football team was a powerhouse, and it seemed as if every boy in town wanted to play on the team someday. Lance decided he'd give both sports a try.

Although Lance wasn't a bad athlete, he wasn't

very coordinated. When he played baseball, he found it hard to catch and hit the ball. He couldn't catch or throw a football very well either, and he wasn't big enough to play on the line. Instead of helping him fit in, playing baseball and football made Lance feel even more left out. He soon gave up on both sports.

But Lance still loved to compete. His mother's example had taught him the value of hard work and determination. He learned that he enjoyed doing things by himself more than as part of a team. He was determined to find a sport he could succeed at and do by himself.

When Lance was in fifth grade, his school held an athletic competition, including a long-distance running race. Lance was determined to win. On the day of the race, he told his mother before he went to school, "I'm going to be a champ."

Lance had never tried running a long-distance race before, but all the time he had spent riding his bike had made him strong and had built up his stamina. Since his mother was away most of the day working, whenever Lance needed to go someplace he always rode his bike. Without being aware of it, he was working out all the time.

When the race started, Lance's classmates expected one of the boys who was a good football or baseball player to win. No one thought Lance would win. But when the race started, Lance settled into a steady pace while most of the other kids started out in a sprint. They soon got tired and slowed down. As they did, Lance passed each one and soon took the lead. The others were already exhausted and eventually stopped trying to keep up with him. He pulled farther ahead with each step and won the race easily, coming home with the first-place ribbon. It was the first time in his life he had ever won anything. He loved the way he felt when one of his teachers handed him the ribbon. He was tired, but happy. He liked the fact that he had won a race that nobody thought he could and that he had done it on his own.

Lance started competing in local organized races and began bringing home ribbons and medals from nearly every race, often beating runners much older than he was. A short time later, at age twelve, Lance joined the local swim club. A lot of kids in Plano belonged to the club, and swimming, like running, was a sport he could do by himself.

At first, Lance was a terrible swimmer. He could stay afloat, but his form was terrible. He tried as hard as he could, but he didn't know the first thing about swimming. He had to practice with kids who were four or five years younger than he was. Lance was embarrassed, but he didn't quit.

Fortunately, swimming coach Chris MacCurdy noticed that Lance always gave his very best. By the end of practice, when most kids were exhausted, Lance was still trying hard. His effort and stamina impressed MacCurdy. With the proper instruction, he believed Lance could become one of his best swimmers and offered to coach him.

With the exception of his mother and other members of her family, no one had ever taken much of an interest in Lance. He quickly responded to the extra attention. Coach MacCurdy took him under his wing and patiently taught Lance how to harness all his energy and how to swim properly.

Every day, Lance noticed he was improving. Within a few weeks, he had progressed enough to train with kids his own age. At first, he was the slowest swimmer in his group. But Lance kept making steady progress, and no one on the swim team worked harder. In a few months, Lance was the fastest swimmer in his group.

But that didn't satisfy Lance. He wanted to be the very best swimmer he could be. When he started competing in meets against swimmers from other clubs, he was determined to win — second place wasn't good enough.

His dramatic improvement continued. Within a year, Lance was one of the best long-distance freestyle swimmers in the state for his age.

Every morning, he woke up before sunrise and rode his bike ten miles from his home to the swimming pool for practice at 5:30 A.M. When practice ended at 7:00 he rode his bike to school. After school, he went back to the pool for more practice before riding his bike back home. Every day, he was riding twenty miles on his bike and swimming six miles!

He began to take swimming more seriously, and he continued to ride his bike whenever he could. One day, when he was thirteen years old, he was hanging around the bike shop and saw a flyer for something called a triathlon. Lance didn't even know what that was, but as he examined the flyer, he realized that a triathlon combined all his favorite sports into one event.

Invented in 1974 by a group of runners who wanted to spice up their training routine, the triathlon is one big race that includes swimming, cycling, and running. Different triathlons set different distances for each of the three elements. In the most famous triathlon, known as the Ironman, the competitors swim 2.4 miles, cycle 112 miles, and then run a full 26.2-mile marathon. The best triathletes finish the Ironman in less than eight hours!

The flyer Lance was looking at described a junior triathlon called the Iron Kid. Although each portion of the race was over a much shorter distance than the Ironman, it was still a big challenge. Lance decided to give it a try.

Lance wasn't sure what to expect, so on the day of the triathlon, he just tried as hard as he could. The swimming leg was first, and all his hard work in the pool with Coach MacCurdy paid off. Lance was one of the first triathletes out of the water. He quickly put on his shoes, jumped on his bike, and started cycling. He soon pulled far ahead of the field.

Race officials were puzzled. They'd never even heard of Lance, yet he was way ahead of the other racers. Most believed he'd started out too fast and would run out of energy during the road race. This is called bonking and often happens to athletes who haven't eaten properly and don't pace themselves. When the body's energy reserves are exhausted it becomes impossible to continue. Many expected this to happen to Lance.

But he was different. All his unofficial training in cycling, running, and swimming had prepared him for the triathlon.

After the cycling race, Lance quickly changed into his running shoes and took off. At the end of the race, he was still running with the same patient, long, loping strides that he had begun with. No one else was even in sight. In fact, some of the other contestants hadn't even finished the bike race yet! Lance won the very first triathlon in which he competed.

Lance felt as if the triathlon had been invented just for him. He started taking the event seriously and trained for the cycling and running portions of the race as hard as he did for swimming. A short time later, he competed in another junior triathlon in Houston that attracted kids from all over Texas. He won that triathlon as well.

The name Lance Armstrong suddenly became well known in triathlon circles. No one so young had ever been so proficient at the sport.

Over the next two years, he competed in triathlons whenever he could. He dominated races for his age group, and when he entered open events, he often beat much older and more experienced athletes.

His involvement in triathlons came at a good time. When Lance was fifteen, his mother and Terry Armstrong divorced. Lance was glad when his step-father moved out. He had never gotten along with him and later told a reporter, "He was totally unfair to my mother." He didn't think his stepfather had treated his mother with respect.

Lance and his mother were on their own again, but this time, Lance knew where he was going.

Chapter Three:
1986–1990

The Kid Graduates

At age fifteen, Lance continued his rapid progress as a triathlete. In the President's Triathlon, a highly competitive race with hundreds of adult competitors from all over the country, Lance finished an incredible thirty-second. Other competitors were shocked. They couldn't believe that someone as young as Lance could even finish the race, much less finish ahead of hundreds of other racers.

But Lance didn't think it was a big deal — he expected to do well. He confidently told a reporter covering the event, "In a few years I'll be right near the top." He fully expected to become one of the best triathletes in the world.

At this point, Lance had outgrown junior events, which were designed for athletes under the age of sixteen, and he lied about his age so he could compete in senior events.

Senior races often paid prize money to the top finishers. In local races, Lance usually finished in the money, and his winnings came in handy. After the divorce, money was tight again, but Lance was able to buy his own clothes and other necessities, including his first car, a used Fiat. In addition, race sponsors were already showering him with all sorts of clothing and sports equipment.

Although Lance was making money, it cost a lot of money to compete. In addition to traveling to and from races and paying for hotels and restaurants, Lance also needed a special triathlon suit that dried out quickly after the swimming portion of the race, high-quality running shoes, and a top-notch bicycle. A race-quality bike can cost as much as four or five thousand dollars. Without the help of sponsors and his own winnings, Lance would have had a difficult time competing. His mother did all she could to help, but there was a limit to how much she could spend.

When Lance turned sixteen, he continued his rapid rise in the sport. In the next President's Tri-

athlon, he finished in fifth place. *Triathlete* magazine named him the sport's Rookie of the Year and
called him "one of the greatest athletes the sport has
ever seen." While his classmates were working at
fast-food restaurants for minimum wage, Lance was
earning almost twenty thousand dollars a year!

Lance couldn't get enough of competition, and in
addition to triathlons and road races, he began competing in cycling events.

Like triathlons and many other sports, cycling is
divided into categories for cyclists of different abilities. Lance skipped right to category one, the top
level, riding for a bike team sponsored by Jim Hoyt,
the man who had sold Lance his first bike. He began
training with Hoyt's team of adult cyclists and even
earned a small salary. Even though he was being
paid, he was still an amateur according to the rules
of the sport. That was important because Lance was
beginning to dream — someday, he hoped to compete in the Olympics. Although the rules have since
changed, at that time an athlete had to be an amateur to be eligible for Olympic competition.

Lance felt invincible. Each day, he spent hours in
training. Winning races had made him very confident,

but he was also only sixteen years old and more than a little careless. He drove his sports car fast, and during training rides, he cycled in and out of traffic taking foolish chances. Even worse, he often trained without wearing a helmet.

One of Lance's favorite training tactics was to try to ride fast enough to time traffic lights so he wouldn't have to stop. Sometimes he'd race through the light even after it had turned yellow.

On one long training run, he barreled toward an intersection at more than thirty miles per hour. The light was yellow as he approached, but just as Lance entered the intersection, the light changed. Lance was going too fast to stop and just kept going.

A woman driving an SUV saw the light turn green and started through the intersection. She accelerated through the crossroads and hit Lance broadside.

The next thing Lance knew he was airborne, tumbling through space. He hit the pavement headfirst and rolled through the intersection, coming to rest against the curb as cars squealed to a stop all around him.

At first, Lance didn't move. People gathered around him, and someone called an ambulance. Lance was bleeding from his head, and the bystanders were afraid he was seriously hurt.

Lance was incredibly lucky. Cycling without wearing a helmet is very dangerous, as even a small accident can cause a severe head injury. But after a few moments, he regained consciousness.

Still, he had to go to the emergency room. He suffered a concussion and a sprained knee, and he had to have stitches in his foot and his head. He could have easily been killed, and his bike was destroyed. The doctor told Lance not to resume training for several weeks and not to compete for six weeks.

But Lance was supposed to race in a triathlon six days later. After a few days, he began to feel better and decided to participate despite his doctor's advice. Amazingly, he showed up at the triathlon and managed to finish third!

Lance and his mother were beginning to realize that he had a bright future as an athlete. The 1988 Summer Olympics were less than two years away, and Lance began dreaming about competing. Although the triathlon wasn't yet an Olympic event, cycling was.

Lance decided to focus on the sport of cycling. He

was getting bored with triathlons, and as he later explained to a reporter, "One problem with the triathlon was that I didn't like swimming all that much. It seemed like everyone went into the water at the same time, thrashed around, and pretty much came out of the water at the same time. Then, on the bike, everyone was drafting, staying close together. So the race basically became a 10K [kilometer] run, which was my worst part. I looked at what I did best, what I liked best. Riding the bicycle. I went with that." There was still nothing he enjoyed more than taking a long ride on his bike, pushing himself to the limit as he pedaled across the Texas plains.

The U.S. Cycling Federation, the organization in charge of cycling in the United States, and sponsors of the national team, became aware of the precocious young cycling star. They began to take an interest in Lance's career. Although making the Olympic team in 1988 wasn't realistic, they viewed Lance as an emerging star who had a great chance to make the 1992 team. Soon, he was being invited to junior races all over the country.

In the United States, the sport of cycling was starting to catch on. An American, Greg LeMond, had won the Tour de France in 1986 and sparked renewed interest in the sport. As more and more people started cycling, manufacturers and other companies began sponsoring teams, and a number of magazines were launched to cover the sport. New competitions were being added constantly. Lance was coming along at just the right time.

Lance was still in high school, but by his senior year, he had little interest in his studies — training and competing were taking up much of his time.

While his mother knew that school was important, she realized that cycling was opening up a whole new world for Lance. It had already changed his life by giving him confidence. She went to Lance's school and tried to explain that he would have to miss some school to compete. While Lance wasn't a great student, he was on pace to graduate with his class.

But school administrators weren't very understanding. They refused to give Lance time off and told her that any absences would be considered unexcused.

In the early spring of 1990, Lance's senior year, he was invited by the Federation to train with the U.S.

National Team and compete in the world championships in the Soviet Union. To do so, he would have to miss nearly two months of school.

Lance and his mother considered the opportunity to compete and travel abroad more important than school. They decided to risk his leaving school, hoping that the school officials would be understanding when he returned.

Training with the national team and competing in the Junior World Championships was a great experience for Lance. Despite his talent, as a cyclist he was still raw. He still had to learn how to race strategically and work on his weaknesses in training.

The Junior World Championship race was a time trial, with each cyclist racing against the clock in a staggered start. Among cyclists, a time trial is called the "race of truth" because the winner doesn't receive any help from his or her teammates. The race tests the ability of the individual.

True to form, Lance broke out at the beginning of the race and had the fastest time over the first few laps. But he paid a price for his exuberance. He didn't pace himself, and as the race wore on, he ran out of steam. However, he still managed to place well, and everyone was impressed — everyone but the administrators of his high school, that is.

When Lance returned to Plano, they told him that if he didn't make up all the work he had missed, they wouldn't allow him to graduate.

Lance was angry. He didn't think it was fair and felt that he was being penalized unnecessarily. He knew it would be impossible to do all the work and maintain his training regimen. His mother finally found a private school that agreed to accept Lance for the final weeks of the semester and would give him credit for the work he had accomplished thus far. He received his high school diploma from his new school.

His high school education may have been complete, but his education as cyclist was just beginning. He still had a lot to learn.

Chapter Four:
1990–1991

National Team

Shortly after graduation, Lance received a phone call from Chris Carmichael, the coach of the U.S. team. Carmichael had been impressed with Lance's performance in the Soviet Union and wanted him to join the national team full time. Carmichael was adding younger cyclists to the team and thinking ahead to the 1992 Olympics.

Lance jumped at the chance; he was tired of living in Plano and eager to go out on his own.

At the same time, former American Olympic cycling coach Eddie Borysewicz convinced Lance to join his professional team, Subaru-Montgomery. When Lance raced internationally, he was a member of the national team, but in U.S. races, he was an amateur member of the Subaru-Montgomery team.

Riding with the national team and with Subaru-

Montgomery was an eye-opening experience for Lance. He had to learn different training methods and to race under a variety of conditions. In Texas, he was accustomed to most races taking place on relatively flat terrain. But internationally, races took place on a variety of courses, ranging from flats to more demanding hills, in all kinds of weather. Road race surfaces included everything from smooth pavement to rough cobblestones. They also took place over longer distances than Lance had experienced.

Lance had a lot to learn in other areas as well, particularly how to behave as part of a team. He still raced and acted like a loner. He wasn't used to being part of a team, and his confidence bordered on obnoxious. As Lance later admitted to a reporter, "The rap was that I was cocky, that I was selfish."

At first, he didn't pay very much attention to what his coaches were trying to teach him. Lance still had to learn the strategic side of cycling because at higher levels, being the fastest cyclist isn't enough to ensure victory. Cyclists have to learn to work with the other competitors. In particular, they have to learn how to draft.

When an object moves forward at a fast pace, it

creates a slipstream behind it. A slipstream is a pocket of air that sucks things forward. Any object that enters the slipstream is pulled along. A cyclist who enters the slipstream, or drafts, behind another cyclist doesn't have to work as hard, because the slipstream pulls him along. Thus, drafting helps conserve energy. Although Lance knew that this was the way he was supposed to race, he often forgot in the excitement of competition.

He paid the price in his first big race after high school, the amateur World Championships in Japan. The 115-mile race took place on a hot, humid day. Coach Carmichael told Lance to stay back, save his strength, and let others attack early in the race. He wanted Lance strong at the end. Privately, Carmichael thought that if Lance did as he was told, he had a good chance to win the race.

But Lance couldn't help himself. Early in the race he felt strong. His legs pumped like pistons, and he effortlessly started passing one rider after another. He soon found himself in front, leading the other cyclists by nearly a minute, a huge lead at that stage of the race.

Lance had made a big mistake. The other cyclists

had let him charge far ahead, knowing that he would have to expend extra energy. When cyclists ride together in a line or larger pack, they help one another conserve strength by breaking the wind. But when cyclists ride alone, they must break the wind by themselves. Although they don't notice it at first, over time the extra effort takes a toll.

At the midway point, just as Lance thought he had the race in hand, he started feeling fatigued. Now each stroke of the pedal took an enormous effort. When the course headed up a small incline, Lance felt as if he were pedaling straight uphill.

His lead dwindled. Lance was soon caught by a pack of thirty cyclists. One by one they started passing him.

Lance tried to fight them off, but he eventually fell into the long line of cyclists, drafting off others. Drafting allowed him to recover some of his strength, and he held on to finish eleventh in the race.

He was disappointed and expected his coach to be mad at him for not following his advice. But Carmichael was pleased. No American had ever finished as high as eleventh in the race, and he liked Lance's fearless approach. However, he also told Lance that if he had followed his advice, he might have won the race. If he ever learned the ins and outs of racing, he had the potential to become a champion. Lance was determined to listen to his coach from then on.

Early in 1991, Lance learned another big lesson. The U.S. National Team was competing in an important ten-stage race in Italy, the Settimana Bergamasca. The field included some of the best cyclists in the world, including Lance's pro team, Subaru-Montgomery.

Compared to time trials, stage races are an entirely different kind of competition. Each team of six to eight cyclists works hard to help one member of the team, their leader, win. Often there are hundreds of cyclists and dozens of teams in a single race. Although stage races often include one or two individual time trials, most stages are long-distance races.

In a long-distance race, team members known as *domestiques* protect the team leader in the pack. They break the wind and allow the leader to conserve energy and draft behind. They also protect the leader from other cyclists, alerting the leader to accidents or other problems on the course. If the leader gets into an accident or has a flat tire, they stop and help so the leader loses as little time as possible and isn't slowed down by members from other teams. Support staff, such as the coaches, trainers, and mechanics, follow the race in a truck.

Stage races take place over a number of days, with a different stage completed each day. Stage races push cyclists to the limit, and many cyclists are often forced to drop out because of injury or fatigue.

Whoever completes all the stages in the lowest overall time is the winner, making it possible to win a race without winning an individual stage. Once a rider gets an overall lead, he or she often rides strategically, allowing cyclists who are far behind in the standings to take the lead and win an individual stage. The leader and the rest of his or her team simply make certain they maintain the overall lead.

Although Lance had started out as a *domestique* on the American team, he quickly became the team leader. He knew his teammates would try their best to help him win.

Early in the race, Lance and one of his Subaru

teammates battled for the lead. Lance was ecstatic to be doing so well, but after one stage, Eddie Bory-sewicz, the coach of the Subaru team, ordered Lance to back off. He wanted Lance to serve as a *domestique* to the Subaru team leader.

Lance was confused. He was riding for the national team and was supposed to try to win, but Borysewicz wanted him to lose.

It just didn't seem right to hold back and let someone else win. Had he been riding for Subaru in the race he would have felt differently. But he wasn't. Even though he knew it might damage his opportunities as a professional, Lance decided to ride for the jersey he was wearing — that of the United States.

The next day, Lance rode hard and broke out with the lead pack. Subaru's lead cyclist couldn't keep up and fell far off the pace. At the end of the day, Lance Armstrong was awarded the yellow jersey, signifying that he was the leader in the race.

But his decision to take the race was controversial. In many European countries, cycling fans and the sporting press follow races and race strategy like Americans follow baseball or football. Lance's decision not to serve as a *domestique* for Subaru was considered arrogant, a betrayal of his team. Italian fans were also disappointed that an Italian cyclist wasn't leading the race, and they took their dissatisfaction out on Lance.

As he clung to the lead over the next few days, Lance and his teammates had to keep one eye on the fans that lined the course. As the American team approached, some fans threw tacks on the road, hoping to give Lance a flat tire and slow him down. Fortunately, Lance and his team managed to avoid the obstacles.

Although the United States dominates international competition in many sports, in cycling they were considered huge underdogs. Teams from much smaller countries were better funded and had better equipment. Compared to some of the European teams, the U.S. National Team looked like a bunch of scruffy kids.

But by the end of the race, even the most hardcore Italian cycling fan couldn't help but be impressed by the toughness of the underdog Americans. Once they realized an Italian cyclist couldn't win, they began pulling for Lance. When he crossed the finish line on the tenth day, he led by more than a minute. The crowd gave him a huge ovation.

Lance was thrilled. The American team had never won a race in Europe before. But they had never had Lance Armstrong as their leader, either.

When Lance stood atop the podium with his teammates, he was almost overwhelmed. For a kid from Texas, he'd come a long, long way.

But his journey had just started. After the race, Coach Carmichael pulled Lance aside. As Lance later wrote in his autobiography, *It's Not About the Bike*, Carmichael told him, "You're gonna win the Tour de France one day."

That would soon become Lance Armstrong's dream.

Chapter Five:
1992
Turning Pro

The notion of winning the Tour de France was something Lance had never given serious thought. He knew that he was still years away from even competing in the Tour. For the time being, his focus was on the 1992 Olympic Games in Barcelona. In the world of cycling, the Olympics weren't nearly as prestigious as the Tour de France, but they were still important. Lance would compete in the 194-kilometer road race.

He trained hard for the race, and some observers considered him a candidate for a medal. In a race like the Olympics, his cocky attitude was considered a sign of strength. No one thought Lance would choke in a big race.

In the months leading up to the Olympics, everything seemed to be going well. Competing with the U.S. team in a stage race in Spain, Lance won three separate stages. Back in the United States, he won time trials in Pittsburgh and Atlanta. Then, in the Olympic trials, he finished second. Everything seemed to be pointing toward a breakout performance in Barcelona.

The U.S. team traveled to Spain more than a month before the Games, practicing on the course around San Sadurni and creating what they hoped would be a winning strategy. Coach Carmichael planned for one of Lance's teammates, Bob Mionske, to forge a breakaway in the middle of the race. Mionske would sprint into the lead and force other cyclists to break away from the pack to keep up with him. Lance was supposed to hang back, then bolt from the pack to the breakaway and pick off cyclists one by one until he was in the lead.

When the day of the race came, Mionske performed his task to perfection. But when Lance tried to move up from the main pack to the breakaway, known as "crossing the bridge," he didn't have the strength to catch up. Try as he might, he just couldn't do it. He finished fourteenth, a strong performance and one of the best ever by an American cyclist in the event. Still, he was disappointed to return to the United States without a medal.

Coach Carmichael blamed himself. "Lance had one bad race all year," he said later. "Unfortunately, it was in the Olympics. I'm responsible for it. There was too much preparation and too narrow a focus. We should have treated it like any other race." He realized that he had worked Lance too hard in the weeks before the Olympics, and his plan had forced Lance to hold back early in the race when he should have been attacking, which was one of his strengths.

But Lance was already looking ahead. Now that the Olympics were over, he could become a professional.

His victory in the Settimana Bergamasca had cost him his place with the Subaru-Montgomery team. Fortunately, his Olympic performance, while personally disappointing, had impressed a number of professional teams. One team, sponsored by Motorola, was particularly interested in Lance.

The Motorola team had been the first American team to compete in Europe, and Coach Carmichael had once ridden for them. When Lance met with team director Jim Ochowicz, he told him simply, "I want to be the best." That's just what Ochowicz wanted to hear. He sent him off to race with his team in Europe. Lance Armstrong was a professional.

Armstrong was thrilled. At the age of twenty-one he was going to be able to do just what he wanted to do — race bicycles all over Europe. For much of the year, there is a race every week. He would eat, sleep, and drink cycling.

His first race was in Spain, the Clásica San Sebastián, a single-day race of more than one hundred miles. Armstrong looked forward to his debut, as did his teammates on the Motorola team.

But the day of the race dawned cold and rainy. Armstrong, accustomed to the milder weather in Texas, hated the rain, and he allowed the weather to affect his performance.

He quickly slipped back into last place and watched the field pull away. Although he tried hard, he just couldn't seem to get his legs to work. Each stroke of the pedals was a struggle. When most cyclists fall far behind, they quit to save their energy for the next race, but Armstrong refused to quit. He didn't want to drop out of his first pro race.

Only 111 cyclists completed the race. Lance Armstrong was the very last one, a full half hour behind the winner and most of the other cyclists. When he reached the finish line, officials were already dismantling the podium, and only a few die-hard fans remained. They jeered him as he finished.

Yet Armstrong's teammates were impressed with his effort. "That night, my teammates realized I wasn't normal," he said later. "I didn't do it [finish] to impress anyone, just to finish. It goes back to my mother. She didn't raise a quitter." She had always advised him to "turn an obstacle into an opportunity. Turn a negative into a positive."

At first, Armstrong thought about quitting and going back to Austin. He was scheduled to go to Zurich, Switzerland, for another race only two days later, but while he was waiting in an airport for his plane, he pondered returning to the United States. He called Coach Carmichael and told him he was thinking about going home.

Carmichael wouldn't hear of it. He told Armstrong he had to learn from his experience, to use his feelings to make himself a better cyclist. Armstrong agreed and got on the plane to Zurich. He would soon follow his mother's advice. As he later admitted, "Finishing last in San Sebastián may have been the best thing that ever happened to me."

He arrived in Zurich with new determination. He promised himself that he would attack at the beginning of the race and try as hard as he could. If that wasn't good enough, then maybe it would be time to quit. But he owed it to himself to give it everything he had.

He did just as he planned. With little thought of race strategy, Armstrong bulled his way into the lead pack and then kept pushing. He finished in second place. He was exhausted, but now he knew that he belonged.

His amazing turnaround, from last place to second, got the attention of the cycling world. Cyclists just didn't make such a dramatic improvement. But as the European cycling community would soon find out, Armstrong wasn't like other cyclists.

"The thing about Lance," Coach Carmichael once said, "is that mentally he doesn't give up." That was another lesson Armstrong learned from his mother. "She gave me discipline," he has said. "She's tough — way tougher than me."

40

Armstrong followed his impressive finish in Zurich with even more impressive performances, winning two races and finishing second in another. Overnight, Lance Armstrong became a household name in Europe.

Beyond his raw talent and determination, Armstrong's personality made him stand out on the European cycling circuit. As an American cycling in Europe, he was a rarity. Unlike the European cyclists, Armstrong didn't know anything about cycling's rich tradition. He didn't know the history of the sport, and he barely recognized cycling's current stars. He didn't give older cyclists much respect, and he didn't behave the way Europeans expected a cyclist to behave.

While most European cyclists were stern and serious, Armstrong wore his emotions on his sleeve. In the midst of a race, if he felt that another cyclist was in his way, he'd yell at him, oblivious of the fact that the cyclist might be doing precisely what his team wanted. He'd mouth off to older, well-respected cyclists, and when he won a race, he'd whoop it up. After races, he rarely hung out with other riders. They thought he was stuck-up.

While the press enjoyed his antics, the other cyclists did not. Armstrong made another enemy in almost every race. His competitors were jealous of his ability, and his attitude gave them another reason to dislike him. Other cyclists and cycling teams began making a special effort to make it hard for Armstrong and the rest of the Motorola team to win.

Race strategy sometimes includes working with cyclists of another team. One team will often help another team attack or block others or try to wear down and tire out an opponent, knowing that the team they help might do the same for them in a later race. But Armstrong and his team received little help.

Other cyclists would sometimes deliberately cut Armstrong off and slow him down. In the midst of the peloton, in which a large group of cyclists ride together, there is generally a lot of pushing and shoving to maintain position, and Armstrong received more than his share. Similarly, the Motorola team found it difficult to find other teams willing to work with them. No one wanted to help Armstrong.

Most of the time, he didn't even realize that what he was doing was wrong. He just didn't know better.

He was still immature, an exuberant, energetic young man with a lot to learn. The brash young American was in a hurry to get to where he wanted to be — atop the cycling world, wearing the yellow jersey to the podium as the champion of the Tour de France. Over the next few years, Lance Armstrong would move closer to his goal — but leave a path of disgruntled opponents in his wake.

Chapter Six:
1993

World Champion

Armstrong's challenge over the next few years would be to take control of his ability, enthusiasm, and energy. Although he was capable of winning almost any race he entered, there were too many races in which he allowed his emotions to take over. He often faded at the end, sometimes wasting the efforts of his teammates. In his heart, he knew he was often the strongest cyclist in the field, but defeat left him feeling frustrated.

Fortunately for Armstrong, his coaches and teammates were patient. They knew him better than he did and realized he had a lot to learn, not just about cycling but about himself. They recognized that his greatest strength was his aggressiveness, but he needed to learn how to channel his emotions on the bike. Most cyclists don't reach their peak until their mid- or late twenties. While he could still win the occasional race, Armstrong was light-years away from being a serious competitor in a demanding event like the Tour de France. As one of his coaches commented, "His ability is like an iceberg. Two thirds of it is just under the surface." Armstrong was just getting started.

Although his background had prepared him for the physical and mental demands of cycling, in many ways Armstrong was still a teenager. He wasn't used to living on his own. He liked to have fun and sometimes didn't get enough rest to put forth his best effort.

Growing up in Texas also hadn't prepared him for the variety of cultures he encountered in Europe. Armstrong was a Texan to the core. He was comfortable there. He liked the wide-open spaces, Mexican food, loud music, and fast cars.

But in Europe, everything was different — the food, the languages, and the way of life. Armstrong wasn't very sophisticated, and at first he resisted taking advantage of wonderful opportunities to learn and experience all the new things that surrounded him every day. Although he was brash and confident when competing in a race, off his bike, in social situations, he felt awkward. In a way, he felt like he had when he was a young boy and first moved to Plano. But this time he couldn't just jump on his bike and ride away from his problems. Armstrong was beginning to realize that to achieve what he wanted as a cyclist meant that he had to grow up and learn to face his problems straight on.

He began to listen to his coaches and his teammates as they gently tried to teach him what he needed to know to succeed. While Armstrong resisted their help at first, he soon began to trust them. For much of his life, Armstrong hadn't needed anyone; now he knew that in order to achieve his goals he had to accept the advice of others. Try as he might, he realized there was no way for him to become the best cyclist in the world all by himself. Isolation was the only thing that was preventing him from reaching the top.

While he worked on his emotions, he found out some interesting things about his physical makeup. As a member of the national team, Armstrong underwent a complete physical at the Human Performance Lab at the University of Texas. He took all sorts of physical and psychological tests to determine just how well suited he was, physically and mentally, to the sport of cycling.

During heavy exercise, such as cycling, the muscles of the human body produce lactic acid. As the amount of lactic acid builds up, the muscles begin to fatigue. The soreness produced after heavy exercise is caused by lactic acid, and there is little an athlete can do to slow or halt its production.

When Lance was tested for lactic acid, the results astounded lab director Dr. Edward Coyle. He described Armstrong as "one in a million, maybe one in ten million." For some reason, Armstrong's muscles produced only one-fourth of the amount of lactic acid that other cyclists produced. That meant that when other cyclists started to feel muscle fatigue, Armstrong did not, explaining his ability to attack and work as such a high level.

As a result, Armstrong is able to push himself much harder than most other athletes. "The doctors just freaked out," he said later. "I just don't seem to generate much lactic acid."

Doctors also discovered that his heart was unusually strong. "Normally, I can ride at a heart rate of

185 beats per minute all the time, and I can sustain above 190," said Lance after the testing. A faster heartbeat allows the blood to deliver more oxygen to his muscles. Few other athletes in any sport can sustain a heart rate much above 170 beats per minute. But Armstrong's heart is so strong that when he isn't cycling, his heart beats only 30 to 35 beats per minute. Most people have a resting heart rate of around 60 beats, and even the best-conditioned athletes rarely have resting heartbeats below 50.

Regardless of how special he was physically, his most impressive quality couldn't be measured in a laboratory: his determination.

The 1993 season demonstrated just how much Armstrong had learned. The U.S. Cycling Federation had developed a series of road races in the United States to help develop American talent. To draw attention to the series, one of the race sponsors offered a bonus of one million dollars if a single cyclist managed to win the one-day race in Pittsburgh, the six-day stage race in the West Virginia mountains, and the 156-mile race in Philadelphia.

The sponsors didn't think it would be possible for one cyclist to win all three events, which required three different skills. To win the bonus, a cyclist would have to be the best sprinter, the best hill climber, and the best stage racer, a nearly impossible combination. But the bonus was all the cyclists could think about. After Armstrong won the first race in Pittsburgh, he set his sights on winning the next two races.

Early in his career, Armstrong had been a weak hill climber. In almost every race, he had lost time in the hills. But he had learned to work on his weaknesses and spent hours training on the hills. In the West Virginia stage race he shocked the field. Not only did he win, but he won the race on the hills. Where everyone had expected him to fall back, he actually increased his lead.

The two wins left Armstrong with a shot at the million-dollar bonus. Even sports fans who knew nothing about cycling were intrigued. No American cyclist had captured the attention of the American public like Armstrong had since Greg LeMond, the first and only American at that point ever to win the Tour de France.

The race in Philadelphia was a 156-mile lap race through the city streets. Armstrong was 1 of 119 cyclists entered in the event, and a crowd of nearly a half million people lined the streets to watch.

Armstrong was finally learning to pace himself. Lap after lap he hung back in the lead pack, letting other cyclists break the wind and expend their energy battling for the lead. With one million dollars at stake, Armstrong kept telling himself to ride a smart race.

With twenty miles remaining, he drew toward the front of the pack just as the race reached the steepest, most difficult part of the course. His recent win in West Virginia had given him confidence during climbs, and because he had conserved his energy, he still felt strong.

As the line of lead riders hit the long hill, Armstrong stood in his seat and let out a long, loud scream as he pushed his body to the limit, furiously driving the pedals of his bike up and down. The other cyclists around him were surprised. Before they had a chance to respond, they saw Armstrong's back pulling away.

There was nothing they could do — Armstrong couldn't be stopped. He powered to the front, flying through the tunnel of fans toward the finish.

Before the race, he'd asked his mother to come to Philadelphia. When he saw her standing alongside the course with one lap to go, he blew her a kiss. Then he roared through the final lap to win the race by the largest margin in history.

Lance Armstrong was a millionaire!

The victory was a breakthrough for Armstrong, a sign that he was on his way to becoming a complete cyclist. When he stood on the podium and received his trophy for winning the race, he broke down and cried, not so much because he had just won a million dollars, but because he now knew it was possible for all his dreams to come true.

Armstrong's next big race would be the Tour DuPont, the American version of the Tour de France and the highlight of the American cycling season. In 1993, this 1,085-mile stage race began in Delaware and continued over the Appalachian Mountains through Virginia and North Carolina. Although the field of competition wouldn't be as deep as in the Tour de France, the Tour DuPont still provided cyclists a stiff challenge. Based on his recent performances, Armstrong was one of the prerace favorites.

In the opening stage, a three-mile time trial

known as the prologue, Armstrong finished second to Mexican cyclist Raul Alcala. Over the remainder of the race, the two cyclists battled for the lead.

Alcala and Armstrong used contrasting approaches. Alcala cycled in a classic European style. He crouched low over his bike, and his upper body remained absolutely still as he deftly maneuvered his bike over the course, constantly taking the shortest route and making certain he stayed as aerodynamic as possible. In contrast, Armstrong was all over the place. He sometimes stood up on his bike to gain power while climbing and weaved in and out of traffic. Cycling fans enjoyed watching the two cyclists fight for the lead.

The Tour DuPont came down to the final stage, a 36.5-mile time trial. Alcala led by only nineteen seconds. The cyclists started at two-minute intervals in reverse order of their placement. Armstrong charged out and was followed two minutes later by Alcala. In order to win, Armstrong had to finish two minutes and twenty seconds ahead of his rival.

As he raced along, his support team kept him aware of Alcala's time. Only six miles into the race, Armstrong received some bad news. Alcala had already gained a full minute on Armstrong to extend his lead. "That was so demoralizing," admitted Armstrong later.

Alcala kept up his relentless pursuit and at the halfway point had Armstrong in sight. At the twenty-three-mile mark he surged past him. Armstrong's chance of victory seemed to disappear.

But it hadn't. When Alcala passed him, his front tire went flat! Armstrong wheeled past. He still had a chance to win.

But Alcala's team was ready. In a timed race, a support vehicle follows trial cyclists. They stopped at his side and had his tire changed in fifteen seconds. Once again Alcala began pursuing Armstrong.

He caught and passed him again only five miles from the end of the race. Armstrong finished second. He was disappointed, but a second-place finish in such a grueling race was still an achievement for the young cyclist.

Armstrong then went to Europe, where he would first compete in the Tour de France and then focus his efforts on the world championship. His first Tour de France would provide a good measure of how far he had come and what remained before him.

Early in the Tour, Armstrong pulled away at the end of a 114-mile stage and sprinted ahead of the pack over the last fifty yards. At age twenty-one, he was the youngest cyclist ever to win a stage in the Tour.

But winning a stage didn't translate into a Tour victory. A few days later, the race entered the mountainous French Alps. Although his climbing ability had improved, Lance was overmatched by the Alps. By the end of the twelfth stage, barely halfway through the race, he was in ninety-seventh place overall, far behind the leaders and with no chance of making up much ground. Rather than continue a futile pursuit and risk injury, Armstrong reluctantly dropped out. Miguel Induráin of Spain won the Tour for the third time.

Armstrong decided to take aim at the world championship in Oslo, Norway, and trained hard prior to the race. Still, few observers gave him much of a chance to win. Induráin was the heavy favorite.

All the best cyclists in the world gathered in Oslo for the race. The cyclists would compete over 14 laps for a total of 257 kilometers — the race would last nearly seven hours.

On the morning of the race, it was raining hard. Armstrong was concerned. The rain reminded him of the weather in his first pro race, when he'd finished last. But Armstrong had grown up a lot since that first race, and he was determined not to let the weather make him lose focus.

When the race started, conditions were terrible. The rain combined with oil on the roads to make them slippery. Riders were sliding all over the course, and accidents were frequent.

Even Armstrong found it impossible to remain upright. Midway through the race, he hit a slick spot, and the bike slid out from beneath him. The rest of the field rocketed by as Armstrong scrambled back aboard his bike.

But as he started pedaling, he couldn't help but smile. His teammates had come to his aid, dropping out of the pack to wait for him. They put him in their draft and helped him work his way back. "It was great to see everybody waiting for me," he said later. With their help he quickly gained the time he had lost.

Armstrong stayed back, knowing that his best chance to win would come at the end of the race. As he said later, "Nothing much happened during those first miles. It was hard for me to get motivated." But he was determined to finish strong.

Over the final laps of the race, he hung with the lead group, keeping his eyes on the great Induráin, waiting to see if the Spanish cyclist would make a move to break away from the pack. But everyone held their positions as if they intended to end the race in an all-out sprint.

Armstrong took a good look at the competition and liked what he saw. The weather had been hard on everyone. The other cyclists in the lead pack looked tired and miserable, and no one seemed eager to break away. "That's when I decided I could win," he recalled later.

On the second-to-last climb of the race, Armstrong decided it was time to make his move. He told himself, "Go like you've never gone before." He jumped up from his seat and pumped up the hill. At the peak, he edged ahead of the leader then went into a coast down the hill, inches ahead. As the second hill approached, he knew he had to open up a lead. The first climb had taken a lot out of him, and if he had to sprint at the end, he was afraid he would be passed.

Once more he rose from his seat and pumped his way up the hill, then began another long descent.

Armstrong focused on hitting each turn perfectly. He kept his foot off the brake and crouched on his bike to retain as much speed as possible. He was afraid to turn his head and glance back. That could slow him down just enough, allowing another cyclist on his back wheel to pass him.

But when he hit the bottom of the hill, he couldn't resist. He glanced back.

No one was in sight. Armstrong was all alone!

At first he was confused. Armstrong thought he may have lost track of the number of laps and made his move too soon. But then he realized he had been right. It was the last lap, and he was way ahead!

He didn't know it until the end of the race, but his teammates had come to his aid, getting in front of the pack and then slowing down, making it hard for others to pass and costing them time.

Over the last few minutes of the race, Armstrong celebrated, pumping his fist as the crowd roared, holding his hands over his head and blowing kisses at the crowd.

He was the champion of the world!

Chapter Seven:
1994–1996

Top of the World

Despite winning the world championship, Armstrong knew that he had still more work to do if he was ever going to win the Tour de France. He even admitted to a reporter shortly after the world championships, "I'm not sure I'm cut out for the Tour. I'm not sure if I'm capable of winning it." For despite winning the world championship and performing well in the Tour DuPont, Armstrong still had a reputation as a "one-day" racer. The top stage races, including the Tour de France, seemed beyond his abilities. Time trials gave him trouble, and although his climbing skills had improved considerably, the Tour had demonstrated that he still wasn't strong enough to climb day after day. Until he improved in both areas, winning the Tour would remain a distant dream.

Lance Armstrong pedals to victory in the 1993 professional men's World Championship Road Race in Oslo, Norway.

With cameras catching all the action, first-place cyclist Armstrong crosses the finish line of stage two of the 1996 Tour DuPont.

Armstrong and his bike: in 1997, it was still uncertain whether he would ride again after being diagnosed and treated for cancer.

Armstrong is a blur of speed as he flies through the nineteenth stage of the 1999 Tour de France.

Leader of the pack: defending champion Armstrong speeds along during the fourteenth stage of the 2001 Tour de France.

The victory draws closer as overall leader Armstrong pedals through and wins the eighteenth stage of the 2001 Tour de France.

V is for Victory! Armstrong wins his third Tour de France.

The 2002 Tour de France winner rides to victory in front of a back-drop of American flags.

Five stands for five Tour de France wins!

Armstrong pedals into the record books as the only person to ever win the Tour de France six years in a row.

Lance Armstrong's Career Highlights

1990:
Second, team time trial; fifth, individual time trial, USCF
   National Road Cycling Championships (Albany, NY)

1991:
First, National Prestige Classic
First, road race; second criterium, team time trial; seventh,
   individual time trial, USCF National Road Cycling
   Championships (Salt Lake City, UT)
Member of the U.S. National Team

1992:
First, First Union Grand Prix
First, three stage-race wins, Vuelta a la Ribera (Spain)

1993:
First, professional road race, World Road Cycling
   Championships (Hamar, Norway)
First, road race, CoreStates USPRO Championships
   (Philadelphia)
Twenty-first, UCI world road rankings

1994:
First, Thrift Drug Classic
Second, Liege-Bastogne-Leige (Belgium)
Twenty-fifth, UCI world road rankings

1995:
First, Clásica San Sebastián (Spain)
First, three stage-race wins, won mountain jersey, Tour DuPont
First overall, Tour of America

1996:
First, five stage-race wins, Tour DuPont
Sixth, individual time trial; twelfth, road race, Olympics
   (Atlanta)
Ninth, UCI world road rankings

1997:
Did not compete because of health problems

1998:
First, one stage-race win, Tour of Luxembourg
Twenty-fifth, UCI world road rankings

1999:
First, won prologue, won stages 8, 9, and 19, Tour de France
Second, King of the Rockies MTB Series (Winter Park, CO)
Seventh (top U.S. rider), UCI world road rankings

2000:
First, won stage 19; sixth, King of the Mountains, Tour de
   France
First, Grand Prix Des Nations (France)
Bronze medal, individual time trial, Olympics (Sydney)
Fourth, UCI world road rankings

2001:
First, four stage-race wins, Tour de France
First, Tour de Suisse (Switzerland)
Fourth, UCI world road rankings

2002:
First, four stage wins, Tour de France
First, Midi Libre
First, one stage win, Dauphine Libere
Third, Championship of Zurich
Second, UCI world road ranking

2003:
First, two stage wins, Tour de France
Eighth, UCI world road ranking

2004:
First, six stage wins, Tour de France
Third, Criterium International

As world champion, Armstrong was in position to earn a lot of extra money by making appearances. Although news of his victory barely registered in the United States, in Europe he was an instant celebrity.

But winning the world championship made Armstrong even more dedicated to making himself a better cyclist. As he said later, his win in Oslo "changed [his] life. The expectation levels grew."

Instead of cashing in, he soon returned to the United States and went to the Olympic Training Center in Colorado Springs. The training center had a state-of-the-art facility designed to test athletes. In addition to medical tests, the technicians at the training center had all sorts of equipment that could evaluate the way Armstrong rode his bike, from how he sat on his seat and held his handlebars to the rate at which he pedaled and the way he leaned when taking the bike into a turn. They could tell him if he was doing anything that was costing him speed.

Over a number of days, Armstrong performed every test he was asked to take. The results were astounding.

While they confirmed that Lance had the physical attributes to succeed, his form was holding him back. He wasn't getting low enough over his seat, and sometimes he was pedaling too fast and at the wrong gear. If he made some changes, he could go faster. Their tests also indicated that if Armstrong made a few small changes to his bike, he could pick up even more speed.

Racing bikes are nothing like the bikes kids ride on the street or on trails. Every part of a racing bike is made to be as light and aerodynamic as possible. They are made of special metals called alloys and cost thousands of dollars.

In 1994, Armstrong began to implement all the changes suggested by the training center. In addition, he and Coach Carmichael changed his training schedule.

Over the first part of the year they "trained through" some races. To help build his stamina, Armstrong often went on a long training ride that ended just as a race was scheduled to begin. Then he'd compete in the race.

But at the end, he wouldn't stop at the finish line. He'd keep going and continue to ride even more extra miles. Other cyclists looked at him as if he were crazy.

At first, his struggles to change his riding style and "train through" races resulted in a string of disappointing performances. Then he started to improve.

Throughout the 1994 season, he began to race much more consistently. He finished second in both the Tour DuPont and the tough European stage race, the Liege-Bastogne-Liege. Ever so slowly he was developing the all-around set of skills needed to win the Tour de France.

His steady improvement continued in 1995. He won the Tour DuPont, won another stage in the Tour de France, and then became the first American to win a World Cup race, winning on the same San Sebastian course where he had finished last in his first pro race. Now, when people discussed the best cyclists in the world, such as Miguel Induráin, they also mentioned Lance Armstrong.

He had finally grown up. He enjoyed living in Europe, where he resided for much of the year. He had learned to speak some German, French, Spanish, and Italian and felt at home all over the continent. He was much more self-confident and took time to explore European culture, visiting art galleries and other cultural sites.

He was now one of the more experienced members of his team, and it was becoming his job to instruct the other cyclists. Armstrong and the top European cyclists got along and treated one another with respect. Now, when he needed help from other cyclists they readily agreed, knowing that Armstrong was likely to return the favor.

In 1996, Armstrong seemed poised to add winning the Tour de France to his cycling résumé. In the spring, he won the prestigious Flèche Wallonne Classic in Belgium and followed that with six second-place finishes in a variety of races. He was consistently among the top finishers in stage races, classics, and time trials and was ranked in the top five in the world rankings of road racers. One magazine referred to him as cycling's "500-pound gorilla," the cyclist no other competitor could afford to ignore. Tony Rominger, the world's second-ranked cyclist, referred to him as "Superman."

In May, Armstrong won his second straight Tour DuPont and set his sights on France and the Summer Olympics in Atlanta. He traveled to Monaco to train. Although he told everyone he was going to concentrate on the 144-mile Olympic road race, scheduled only ten days after the end of the Tour, everyone knew that once the Tour de France started, if Armstrong sensed that he had a chance to win, he would be hard to stop. Miguel Induráin was the favorite, but if he faltered, Armstrong seemed destined to challenge him.

When the Tour started, he felt better than he had ever felt in his life. But he ran into problems almost immediately. He caught a cold, which quickly turned into bronchitis. He was congested and found it hard to breathe.

Although bronchitis is only a minor health problem, for a world-class cyclist it can be devastating. If a cyclist can't breathe freely it becomes almost impossible to compete. After gasping for his breath for a few days, Armstrong reluctantly dropped out. His back was aching, and he also had a sore throat. With the Olympics so close, there was no sense pushing himself and harming his Olympic chances.

But in Atlanta he still felt weak. Despite being a heavy favorite to win the gold, a medal eluded him. He finished sixth in the time trial and twelfth in the road race.

Still, Armstrong wasn't concerned. He thought he

had a touch of the flu. His performance in the first part of 1996 marked him as one of cycling's biggest stars. Already, he was favored to take his first Tour de France in 1997. He signed a big endorsement contract with the sporting-goods manufacturer Adidas and left his Motorola team to ride for the French team Cofidis, signing a two-year contract worth more than 2 million dollars. Financially secure, he moved into a spectacular house on the shores of Lake Austin in Austin, Texas.

Life was good. On September 18, when he celebrated his twenty-fifth birthday, Lance Armstrong was on top of the world. Apart from the occasional cold, it seemed as if nothing could stop him.

Chapter Eight:
1996–1997

Cancer

A world-class athlete like Lance Armstrong knows his body better than most people know theirs. He pays attention to every little ache and pain, aware that they can sometimes indicate the beginning of a larger problem.

In September of 1996, Armstrong felt a dull pain in one of his testicles. He thought it might have something to do with the flu he had, that perhaps a small infection had caused his glands to become inflamed.

A few nights after his birthday, Armstrong got a bad headache. It went away a day later, but he had never had such a bad headache. A few days later while talking on the phone, he had a severe coughing attack. He went into the bathroom and discovered that he was coughing up blood.

Now Armstrong was worried. Coughing up blood is usually an indication of a serious health problem.

Lance called a doctor, but after a quick examination, his doctor didn't find anything wrong. He told Armstrong that he might have been bleeding from his sinuses.

But when Armstrong woke the next day, his aching testicle had swollen to three times its normal size and was extremely painful. He went back to the doctor and spent the whole day undergoing a series of tests.

With each examination, Armstrong grew more concerned. No one was telling him what was wrong, and when they ordered him to have a chest X ray, he didn't understand why.

But at the end of the day he met with the doctor. He was shown an X ray of his lungs, and there were white spots all over it.

"It looks like testicular cancer," said the doctor. The cancer in his testicles had already metastasized, or spread, into his lungs. The doctor told Armstrong he should have surgery as soon as possible.

Armstrong was in shock. As an athlete, he was accustomed to overcoming obstacles through hard work and determination. Cancer was something he wouldn't be able to fight by himself. He knew the disease was serious and that it could kill him.

He didn't know what to do. He was certain his career was over and that he would never be able to race again. He went home and called his closest friends, his girlfriend, his agent, and several teammates and told them the bad news. He was so upset that he asked a friend to call his mother for him. Everyone who lived nearby came over and gave Armstrong their support.

The next morning, he went to the hospital for surgery. A surgeon removed his testicle in a three-hour operation, and other doctors took blood and performed more tests.

It seemed as if every test delivered more bad news. Doctors rank the severity of cancer according to stages. Stage one is the least dangerous because it means the cancer is confined to one area, and it is often relatively easy to treat. Stage three means the cancer has spread. Lance had stage three cancer. In addition to the tumors in his lungs, Lance also had cancer in his abdomen. It was spreading very quickly and getting worse every day.

No one could tell him why he got cancer. Although scientists learn more about the disease every day, there is no definitive explanation as to why one person gets cancer and another doesn't. Although some activities, such as smoking, are known to cause cancer, Armstrong had lived a healthy life. He was in great shape.

He spent the next week recovering from surgery and getting his life in order before beginning twelve weeks of chemotherapy. He learned as much as he could about his disease so he could understand what was happening to him. Just before he began the treatments, he held a news conference and announced to the world that he had cancer. "I'm determined to fight this disease," he said, "and I will win." But he also knew it would take a lot more than saying those words to survive.

Chemotherapy is intensive treatment with drugs that are given to a patient directly into the bloodstream through a device called an IV. The drugs are so powerful that they usually make the patient feel very ill, for while the drugs kill the cancer cells, they also kill other cells in the body, such as the red blood cells that carry oxygen. Many cancer patients lose their hair because the fast-growing hair cells that push new hair out of the scalp are killed by the drugs. Most cancer patients undergo chemo in stages, spending several weeks in treatment and then stopping to recover for a week or two before resuming.

Even though he had cancer, Armstrong was fortunate in some ways. Testicular cancer is among the most treatable forms of the disease. Medical advances over the last twenty-five years have dramatically improved the chances for survival. Even in Armstrong's advanced condition, his doctors said his chances for recovery were good.

Fortunately, chemotherapy didn't make him feel too bad at first. In fact, he started riding his bike again as soon as the wounds from his surgery healed. As it had when he was a child, cycling kept his mind off his problems and made him feel better. As long as he could still ride, thought Armstrong, he was still alive.

But the news just kept getting worse. First, he learned that he didn't have any health insurance. When he had switched teams, from Motorola to Cofidis, he had to change insurance. His new insurance didn't cover preexisting illnesses, and even though he didn't know it, he had the cancer before he switched over. On top of everything else, Armstrong had to worry about paying for all his treatments. Although he had quite a bit of money saved up and a disability insurance policy, he knew that the treatments could wipe him out financially.

As he learned more about the disease, he began to visit other doctors. They took a look at his records and decided to look for more cancer in his brain. They found two tumors. Now they told him his chances for survival didn't look very promising.

Lance went all over the country consulting with doctors, trying to find the best treatment for his kind of cancer. He finally decided to put his life into the hands of a team of doctors led by Dr. Craig Nichols at the University of Indiana. They were more optimistic about his chances for recovery. Moreover, they believed they could cure him and leave him healthy enough to continue his cycling career. Some drug treatments cause lung damage, and radiation therapy, also sometimes used to treat cancer, can cause other long-term health problems and leave people weak. Armstrong's doctors decided that it was best to treat Armstrong with chemotherapy and to remove the brain tumors surgically.

At least that's what they told him. Years later, Armstrong's doctors admitted to him that they were surprised that he had survived. But they never let him know how sick he really was, knowing that his attitude would be critical to his recovery.

Armstrong found the idea of brain surgery frightening. Although the tumors were on the outside of his brain, there was still a chance that their removal could harm the areas of his brain that controlled his sight and coordination.

But Armstrong maintained a great attitude. His fans sent him thousands of get-well cards and e-mails, giving him advice and helping to keep up his spirits. Each one helped, and his friends and family also gave him their support.

Doctors aren't sure why, but a person's attitude often seems to have an impact on the way they respond to illness. Armstrong was remaining positive. Although he worried about what might happen to him, he didn't dwell on negative thoughts. He kept imagining his life *after* he had regained his health and was riding his bike, winning races, and spending time with the people he cared about.

In an odd way, Armstrong was even beginning to

enjoy his fight against cancer. He had felt like an underdog his whole life and loved proving that he could do something no one else thought he could. He had thrived knowing the odds were against him and that he'd have to struggle. He approached his illness the same way.

The brain surgery went much better than the doctors had expected. The tumors had already stopped growing, and Lance's vision and coordination were unaffected by the operation. Then he had to resume chemotherapy.

As he went through additional cycles of chemo, his body finally began to feel the effects of the treatment. He began to feel sick. He would throw up and sometimes be unable to get out of bed, and his hair fell out.

After each cycle of treatment, he'd slowly begin to feel better. He received an invitation to attend a race in Austin as a spectator. Instead — and incredibly — Armstrong actually participated in the brief two-man time trial. The race was on November 10, barely three weeks after his surgery.

However, it soon became impossible for Lance to ride his bike at all. As his chemo resumed, he grew weaker and weaker. He had so few red blood cells that his muscles just couldn't get enough oxygen.

That's when Armstrong made an interesting discovery. Before he had gotten sick, he'd never thought much about why he liked cycling. Ever since he started to compete, it had simply been the means to an end, the way he earned his living. Now he began to realize that he really liked just being on the bike, going someplace and feeling the wind on his face. For the first time in his life, he began to appreciate what he was able to do. Every day he was learning more about himself and gaining perspective on his life.

When the final round of chemo ended, Armstrong returned home and tried to regain his strength. He didn't know what the future held for him.

Cofidis, his French team, was threatening to cancel his contract. And Armstrong wasn't sure if he could become a world-class cyclist again, or even if he wanted to. He had learned so much about cancer that he pondered going to college to become a cancer doctor.

What energy he had he put into helping others fight the disease. He started a foundation to support cancer charities and spoke out publicly to encourage men to perform self-examinations for testicular cancer and seek medical help if they discovered any abnormalities. Although the disease is rare, it is the second most common form of cancer among men ages eighteen to thirty-four.

For the next year, Armstrong slowly regained his strength as his body bounced back from the effects of chemotherapy. He periodically had to be tested to see if the cancer had returned. Each time, the results came back clear.

He started cycling again, not to resume racing, but just for pleasure. He soon realized that nothing made him happier.

Finally, nearly a year after he was first diagnosed with cancer, Armstrong's doctors told him he could consider himself cancer-free. The chance that the disease would return was remote.

So were the chances that Lance Armstrong would once again become a world-class cyclist. But after giving it some thought, he decided he would give it a try.

Chapter Nine:

1997–1998

A New Stage

Armstrong's agent contacted Cofidis and told them that Armstrong was ready to resume training, but his team wasn't very enthusiastic. They offered him only a small contract laden with incentives if he managed to resume his previous form.

Most other racing teams were even less enthusiastic. Most didn't even want to meet with Armstrong and his agent.

Although Armstrong looked healthy, he had lost nearly 20 pounds after his illness, dropping from 175 to 158 pounds. His physical strength had always set Armstrong apart from other cyclists, and now his strength seemed to have disappeared. Besides, to become the cyclist he had been before cancer, Armstrong would have to be at 100 percent. If he came back and was only 95 percent of the cyclist he was before, he'd be just another rider in the middle of the pack. *Domestiques* earned only forty or fifty thousands dollars a year. Armstrong didn't want to be a *domestique,* and no one was going to offer him a contract to be a leader again.

However, a new American team, the U.S. Postal Service squad, was willing to take a chance.

Lance spent November and December training in the United States, and then went to Europe to ride with his new team.

Armstrong was confident that he'd eventually resume his place as one of the best cyclists in the world. But even he didn't realize how hard it would be.

In a way, he was an entirely new person, not only physically but also in other ways. While recovering, he had met a woman, Kik, who would soon become his wife. His priorities were changing. So while he was adjusting to racing again, he was also adjusting to sharing his life with someone else.

Armstrong underestimated just how hard it would be to adapt to the racing lifestyle again. At times he raced well, but at other times he just couldn't find a reason to keep going. While he had recovered physically, he wasn't psychologically ready to compete.

In the back of his mind he was worried that his cancer might return. After a string of disappointing performances, he dropped out in the middle of a race. He returned to the house he and Kik shared in France and said he was going back to the United States. They quickly packed and were back in Austin before anyone knew they had left Europe.

He told everyone that he was going to retire. Everything that had once come so easily was now a struggle. Armstrong was frustrated and angry. He tried to enjoy life without cycling, but he was actually ashamed to have quit.

His agent and cycling friends convinced him to hold off on making an announcement that he was retiring. They wanted him to ride in the race sponsored by his foundation and race in the U.S. National Pro Championships. They told Armstrong he owed it to his fans to give them a chance to see him one more time.

Armstrong fell for it. He didn't know that they were trying to trick him into getting back on his bike. They all thought that Armstrong had tried to return to cycling a little soon, before he was really prepared.

He started cycling again so he wouldn't embarrass himself at the foundation race and in the U.S. Pro Championships. Before he knew it, he had rediscovered his love of the sport. He and Kik got married, and when he finished fourth in the pro championships, he knew he was ready. Instead of preparing to retire, he began to plot his comeback.

Armstrong and his wife moved back to Europe for the racing season. He focused on time trials and classics, building his strength. Although he didn't experience immediate success, when he did fail it didn't bother him. He just rode harder the next time and chalked it up to a bad day.

Then he started winning, collecting three first-place finishes before ending the season with a fourth-place finish in the grueling Tour of Spain, the Vuelta. At the end of the season, he received a message from the director of the U.S. Postal Team. It read, "You'll look great on the podium of the Tour de France next year." Armstrong couldn't help but smile when he read it. If the director thought Lance was ready to resume stage racing, then Lance knew it was true. He decided to focus all of his efforts on winning the 1999 Tour de France.

Armstrong spent the winter training in the United States. During those months, Kik became pregnant. That made Lance look forward to 1999 even more. The knowledge that he was going to have a child made him all the more committed to succeeding.

He returned to Europe in the spring to race but kept struggling, taking several bad falls and finishing in the middle of the pack.

But Armstrong wasn't worried. He didn't care that he wasn't winning races in March and April. The only race he cared about took place in July — the Tour de France.

Armstrong studied the course and went on long training runs over many stages of the race. He climbed hills relentlessly, realizing that hills were now one of his strengths and that the Tour would be won or lost in the mountains.

Incredibly, over months of training, Armstrong learned that having cancer had actually made him a better cyclist. The loss of nearly twenty pounds make him quicker on the flats and made it easier for him to climb. As the race approached, Armstrong grew confident.

The sport of cycling was at a crossroads. The

1998 Tour de France had been marred by charges that some top cyclists had cheated by using illegal performance-enhancing drugs. Several cyclists had been suspended, and others decided to boycott the race after their integrity had been questioned. For the first time in years, there was no clear favorite.

Prerace speculation identified American Bobby Julich, who'd finished third in 1998, as a favorite, along with Michael Boogerd and Abraham Olano. A few prerace stories mentioned Armstrong because of his fourth-place finish in Spain in 1998, but he had raced so little in 1999 that no one was quite sure if he was ready for the Tour. Most racing fans dismissed his chances entirely. After all, Armstrong hadn't been a threat to win the race before cancer. How could he win the Tour de France now?

Only Armstrong knew the answer to that.

Chapter Ten:
1999

Comeback

Publicly, Armstrong talked down his chances of winning. "I want to think about being in the top ten," he said. "I'm coming into the Tour knowing I've only finished the race once."

Even the best riders found finishing the race a challenge. Of the nearly two hundred cyclists who begin the race each year, only about two-thirds finish. Many are hurt, get sick, or give up when the race moves into the mountains.

But privately, Armstrong was cautiously optimistic about his chances. During training, he had set record times over some stages of the race. He didn't think any other cyclist had worked harder or was better prepared for the Tour.

The race began with the prologue, an eight-kilometer time trial. The prologue is designed to sort the cyclists out for the start of the race. The faster finishers are allowed to begin at the front of stage one, ensuring they will get off to a good start and won't get bogged down in traffic. Although the time of the prologue doesn't count in the overall race results, it's important to get a good start.

Cyclists started at three-minute intervals. Armstrong was able to communicate with his team director over a radio he wore during the race. He left the starting line knowing that several others cyclists had already broken the all-time prologue record.

Five kilometers into the race was a big hill. Armstrong knew he would have to take the hill at full tilt, keep his momentum, and then power to the finish because after the hill, the course still continued up a slow incline.

Armstrong hit the hill trailing the leader by several seconds. He kept low and pushed as hard and fast as he could.

When he crossed the finish line, he looked at the clock. Eight minutes and two seconds! A new record! No other cyclist bettered his mark. He would start the race in first place, wearing the special yellow jersey that identifies the leader.

He was ecstatic. "I think I'm a better bike rider than I was before," he said. Miguel Induráin, who was no longer racing, said he believed Armstrong could win the race. That gave him even more confidence. But there were still three weeks of racing and nearly two thousand miles to go.

It is virtually impossible to wear the yellow jersey the entire race, and no cyclist wins every stage. Each stage is a minirace of its own and worth bonus money, so even cyclists with no chance of winning the Tour will try hard to win a stage. Still, Armstrong knew he had to remain near the front when the race entered the mountains.

He held the yellow jersey for two days before falling back, but he was able to stay with the lead riders. On stage eight he made his move.

The race was a thirty-four-mile time trial, a "race of truth" that promised to separate the weak from the strong. Armstrong was familiar with the course. During training, he had ridden it twice. On the morning of the race, he rode it again. He remembered there was one bad turn and studied it closely. It was raining, and the roads were slick. He reminded himself to be careful.

He left the starting line three minutes after Abraham Olano, one of the favorites. Sure enough, Olano crashed on the curve and lost valuable time. Armstrong handled the turn with ease, and midway through the race, he caught and passed Olano. The Spanish cyclist had never been passed in a time trial before.

Armstrong blew away the field and led by more than two minutes when the race entered the mountains. But when he was asked about his chances, he reminded the press that even five-minute leads meant little once the stages in the mountains began. His lead could evaporate quickly if he had a bad day or crashed and was injured. He was in good position, but the race wasn't over. On the climbs in the mountains, he knew he would sometimes have to slow down to less than ten miles an hour. On the downhill portions, he would rocket along at speeds approaching seventy miles per hour. Armstrong knew a crash could be disastrous, even deadly.

Armstrong and his teammates approached stage nine strategically. The U.S. Postal Team planned to help Armstrong draft through the first climbs to save his energy. He planned to attack over the final miles of the stage during the final ascent of 6,600 feet up a mountain in the French Alps.

Armstrong and his team focused on staying near the front and staying out of trouble. On the last climb, Armstrong made his move.

He picked up his pace and ever so slowly began to close on the cyclists in front of him. One by one he picked them off, and with each stroke of his pedals, he drew closer to the leaders. They all looked exhausted, but Armstrong still felt strong. He passed them like they were standing still and then kept going. By the time he reached the finish line, he had increased his lead in the Tour to more than six minutes. "I wanted to answer the question about my ability to climb," he said. He did more than that.

His big win broke the spirit of the other cyclists. Olano, in second place, admitted, "I can only hope he falters. Now I will ride to defend my place on the podium." By that, he meant finishing either second or third. He already knew the top spot would belong to Armstrong.

The big lead allowed Armstrong to race defensively as the Tour continued through the Alps and into the Pyrenees, another mountain range. All he had to do was stay ahead. When other teams and riders went out on a breakaway, he didn't have to give chase. Instead, he simply kept track of who was in second place and made certain he didn't allow his lead to shrink. Armstrong's teammates took turns breaking the wind and shielding him from other cyclists. His lead held.

But as it looked more and more likely that Armstrong would win, some cyclists and members of the press started attacking him. They began to question whether he could perform so well after cancer without the help of illegal drugs.

The charges made Armstrong angry. He knew that his performance wasn't due to any pill. Because of the scandal of the previous year, everyone had to be tested for drugs. Armstrong passed every test.

He decided it was time to make a statement. When the race came down from the mountains, there was a time trial of just over thirty-five miles. Unless Armstrong crashed, it would be impossible for another rider to gain much time on him. It made sense for him to ride conservatively.

But Armstrong had already won two time trials. He wanted to win a third. In the history of the Tour it had been done only three times before.

Armstrong pushed himself hard and completed the course in just over one hour and eight minutes, winning the race by nine seconds and opening up an insurmountable overall lead of nearly eight minutes.

Barring a disaster, it would be impossible for another cyclist to catch him. The final stage of the Tour is an easy, flat ride into Paris, and according to tradition, the cyclists all take it easy until they draw within sight of the Eiffel Tower. Then, once they reach the Arc de Triomphe, there is a quick ten-lap sprint before a final ride down the Champs Élysées, the most famous boulevard in Paris.

The weather was beautiful, and large, boisterous crowds packed the route. Lance rode in the midst of the *peloton,* surrounded by his teammates, basking in his victory, and for once during the race, actually paying attention to the sights and sounds of the Tour. For the first time, he could relax.

Armstrong soaked in every minute. When he crossed the finish line, a crowd of well-wishers, which included nearly all his close friends, swarmed him.

"I never expected to be here," he said. "Even in my first career, I never had plans for this."

He had beaten cancer and won the Tour de France.

Chapter Eleven:
1999-2000

A Special Win

When Armstrong returned to the United States, he couldn't believe the reception he received. Overnight, he had become a celebrity. People considered him a hero.

All of a sudden, people were talking about cycling in the United States. Many observers considered his victory as shocking as if a French football team won the Super Bowl. Not since Greg LeMond had won the Tour de France three times between 1986 and 1990 had the American public paid attention to cycling.

Armstrong basked in the attention. Apart from making him wealthy with a host of endorsement opportunities, he had the chance to speak to millions of people about testicular cancer. Nearly every time Armstrong went on television or the radio and spoke about the disease, someone recognized the symptoms and sought medical help. Had Armstrong never had cancer himself, many of these men might have died.

When Lance was asked if he would have rather had the experience of winning the Tour or of surviving cancer, he answered, "Survive cancer." Now that he was free of the disease, he understood that the experience had made him a better person. He was more comfortable with himself than he had ever been before he was ill.

That fall, Kik Armstrong gave birth to a son, Luke, making Armstrong a father. He was beginning to feel as if his life was complete.

But his cycling career was far from over. If anything, winning the Tour and becoming a father made him even more motivated. He wanted to prove that his victory in 1999 wasn't a fluke.

Some critics charged that the field of cyclists in 1999 had been weak, with several top cyclists missing the race because of injury or protests over the drug scandal. In the spring of 2000, Armstrong set his sights on winning the Tour again.

But while on a training run in the Pyrenees,

Armstrong's race nearly ended before it even started. As he pedaled slowly up a long, steep climb at only a few miles an hour, he started to sweat heavily and took off his helmet, intending to put it back on when he began his high-speed descent. But Armstrong was so focused on the ride that he forgot to do that.

As he gained speed down the narrow road, his front tire hit a rock and went flat. The wheel twisted, and he lost control of the bike. As it careened off the road and Armstrong flew through the air, the only thing he saw was a brick retaining wall.

Crash! Armstrong hit the retaining wall head-on. Everything went black.

Armstrong was dazed. Fortunately, a couple of doctors happened to see the crash and rushed to his side. They kept him still and called an ambulance.

Armstrong was extremely lucky. Apart from some bumps and bruises and a concussion, he was okay. But he easily could have been killed. He was embarrassed that he had forgotten to put his helmet back on. That small mistake could have cost him his life.

Armstrong resumed training a few days later. Apart from riding his bike, he also studied the course closely. Although the Tour always travels around France in a rough circle, the actual route of the course varies each year. In 2000, the Tour would go counterclockwise, rather than clockwise as it had in 1999.

Race officials had also made a few changes. Instead of a short time trial, the prologue was now a ten-mile race. It would provide a much tougher test for the cyclists and made it even more important for Armstrong to do well.

He did do well but finished second, moments behind his teammate, David Millar, a young cyclist many observers were calling the next Lance Armstrong. Like the young Armstrong, he was full of energy and rode with a devil-may-care attitude. He blistered the course to take the yellow jersey at the start of the race. Although Armstrong was disappointed to lose, he was pleased to have been defeated by a teammate.

Over the first few stages, Armstrong raced well but couldn't manage to gain the lead. Once again, he knew the race would be decided in the mountains.

Armstrong started the 127-mile tenth stage in sixteenth place, just under six minutes behind the leader, but none of the cyclists ahead of him were considered serious contenders. The other top cyclists were even farther behind. He was confident he could soon take command.

The weather was terrible. The temperature hovered around 45 degrees, and rain fell in sheets, pelting riders in the wind. Earlier in Armstrong's career such conditions would have bothered him. But years of training had hardened him to the weather. After the race he said, "I like these conditions."

Armstrong was relentless. One by one he passed other riders until he found himself in a pack with three of his biggest challengers — Jan Ullrich, Alex Zülle, and Marco Pantani. Another pack was just ahead. A single cyclist led the stage, but Armstrong already led him by a comfortable margin.

He had to make sure he didn't lose time to his rivals. Pantani attacked first, sprinting ahead, trying to leave the rest of the pack behind.

Armstrong went right after him. Zülle and Ullrich faded.

Pedaling hard, Armstrong drew alongside his rival and then accelerated, a look of determination on his face. Pantani grimaced and tried to keep up, but with each stroke, he fell farther behind.

Armstrong just kept going, and within a few miles, he caught and passed the remaining pack of riders, which included Richard Virenque, who was widely acknowledged as the best mountain cyclist in the world. "Armstrong came on like a plane at the end," said the French cyclist.

Armstrong finished second in the stage, and incredibly, he had picked up enough time to take the lead. In one day, he went from being six minutes behind to leading by nearly four minutes. The yellow jersey was his!

The other cyclists tried everything to stop him. They knew if they didn't catch him soon, it would be too late.

In the next few stages, they ganged up on Armstrong. The U.S. Postal Team was having a hard time in the mountains, and the other teams tried to keep Armstrong separate from his teammates, knowing the race would be that much more difficult for him if he was forced to ride alone. But try as they might, no one could make up any ground on Armstrong.

But in stage sixteen, Armstrong made a rare mistake. In an earlier stage, he had backed off at the end and allowed Marco Pantani to win. Armstrong meant to do so as a gesture of respect, but Pantani misinterpreted the gesture. He thought Armstrong was patronizing him. In stage sixteen the Italian rider foolishly decided to make Armstrong pay.

Pantani bolted far ahead of the beginning of the race. Although Armstrong and his team thought Pantani had gone out too fast and would be unable to maintain his torrid pace, he was such a talented cyclist that they had to stay close.

Pantani wasn't racing to win the Tour — he was just racing to destroy Armstrong. It almost worked.

Sure enough, Pantani ran out of steam in the middle of the race and then dropped out of the tour, but he left Armstrong exhausted. With just a couple of miles remaining, Armstrong bonked and ran out of energy. Cyclist after cyclist passed him as he struggled to the finish. "Today was the hardest day of my life on a bike," he said after the race.

He still led the race by some four minutes, and with only four stages remaining, Armstrong was still in good shape. But he had given Ullrich some hope.

But Ullrich wasn't up to the task. Over the next couple of stages, Armstrong put more space between himself and his rival. Once again he pedaled into Paris as the winner.

When Armstrong crossed the finish line, he was greeted by an enormous crowd, which this time included hundreds of Americans waving the Texas flag and cheering. When he took the podium, he carried his young son.

He took a great deal of satisfaction from the win. "I consider this a confirmation of last year," he said. "They were all here," he added, referring to the top competitors. "It [the win] is a vindication.

"This one is even more special than last year, partly because of this little guy," he said, in reference to his son.

This time most observers gave Armstrong full credit for the win. "Armstrong is a worthy champion," said Jan Ullrich. "He was the strongest man, and he met our every attack. He earned his victory."

But there was one more title Armstrong wanted to add to his collection before the year was over — an Olympic gold medal in Sydney, Australia. Thus far, that was all that had eluded him. He remained in France to train.

One day on a training ride, Armstrong ripped

around a hairpin turn he had taken hundreds of times before. There wasn't much traffic on the road, and he wasn't being very careful. But when he made the turn, there was a car directly in front of him. He collided with the car head-on, flew over it, and landed on his head in the middle of the road.

This time he was wearing a helmet. He didn't think he was hurt and went home, but the next day he was in such pain that he had to go to the hospital. He had broken vertebrae in his neck.

The injury kept him from training, and he went to Sydney a little out of shape. He finished fourteenth in the road race but bounced back to take a bronze medal in the time trial. He had tried as hard as he could, though, and wasn't disappointed.

By this point in his life, Armstrong knew that while winning was nice, other things were more important.

Chapter Twelve:
2001–2003

Three, Four, Five

Only a few cyclists in history have won more than two Tours. Bernard Hinault and Eddy Merckx each won the race five times and are considered two of the greatest cyclists of all time. With another victory in the Tour, Armstrong would be on his way to joining their select company.

The 2001 Tour would provide the most difficult test of his career, and Armstrong would deliver one of his most remarkable performances.

He once again focused his energy on the Tour. Although he didn't ignore other races, he used them to prepare and gauge his progress. In the months before the Tour, Armstrong proved that he was taking a third try at a win seriously by winning the Tour de Suisse. Meanwhile, others were still getting into shape.

But Armstrong realized he was getting older. More than ever before, race strategy would be important.

Over the opening stages of the Tour, Armstrong held back, once again conserving his energy for the mountains, where he still felt that he could take command of the race. But Armstrong wasn't the only cyclist racing strategically.

In the eighth stage, a pack of more than a dozen cyclists broke free of the *peloton* on a breakaway. Although all but a few of the cyclists were sprinters with no real chance to win the Tour, several were legitimate contenders.

Armstrong and his teammates had a decision to make. They could go on a breakaway of their own and try to stay near the lead pack or conserve their energy within the *peloton*.

The breakaway pack opened up a huge lead, while the *peloton* with Armstrong and his teammates fell far back. By the time Armstrong realized how big the lead had grown, it was too late to do anything about it.

The pack finished more than a half hour ahead of the *peloton*, the greatest gap in Tour history. Armstrong ended the day in twenty-fourth place, more than thirty-five minutes behind leader Sean O'Grady. Even though O'Grady wasn't considered a serious contender, Armstrong was behind several others who were. In addition, no one had ever fallen so far behind and still won the Tour. Then again, no one was quite like Lance Armstrong. But this time he would have a mountain of a deficit to make up in the mountains of France.

He made his big move in stage ten. For most of the race, Armstrong and Jan Ullrich kept pace with each other and slowly moved past slower riders, each picking up valuable time.

But Armstrong knew that Ullrich would eventually prove to be his biggest challenge. The cyclist was strong, and Armstrong knew that in order to beat him he would have to outsmart him.

Armstrong dropped back, out of sight of Ullrich. A motorcycle covering the race for French television drew close to him and trained their camera on Armstrong's face. Viewers saw him gasping for air as if he were struggling. He was breathing heavily with his mouth wide open.

Armstrong knew that the German team would be watching television coverage in their support car and would pass along word of his condition to Ullrich's coach. That's exactly what happened. Ullrich's coach contacted his rider on the radio and told him that his fast pace had broken Armstrong. This was his chance to put Armstrong away and win the Tour!

Ullrich and his team pedaled harder. He wanted to increase his lead over Armstrong and make him think he couldn't win.

But Armstrong wasn't struggling at all. He wasn't tired. He actually felt strong. As soon as the camera left him, he stopped acting as if he was tired and accelerated, slowly creeping up on Ullrich.

On the final climb, Armstrong made his move. He saw that Ullrich was beginning to weaken. Armstrong was calm and composed, settled back in his seat, and pedaling in a steady rhythm, drawing closer to Ullrich every second.

All of a sudden, he was alongside his challenger. Armstrong turned his head, looked his opponent in the eye for a moment, and then broke away.

Ullrich looked as if he'd just seen a ghost! He had no idea Armstrong was still in contention in the race. He thought he had left him far behind.

He started pedaling furiously, but after only a few

strokes, he realized it was hopeless. He and his team had been fooled!

His shoulders slumped, and he threw off his radio headphones in disgust. Armstrong finished nearly two minutes ahead of Ullrich, raising his hands in triumph as he crossed the finish line to win the stage. He had zoomed all the way up to fifteenth place, gaining an incredible nine places in one day.

Armstrong was beaming after the race. "This was a very special stage," he said. "A mystical stage. Sometimes you have to play a little game," he added with a smile. "We decided to play poker a bit. I knew they were watching on TV." Incredibly, Armstrong's own radio was broken, and he had raced without it for most of the stage.

Ullrich was crushed. "Maybe Lance will have a breakdown," he said. "I have not lost the Tour." Although that's what he was saying, it didn't sound like he believed his own words.

Armstrong kept pushing. Two stages later, he passed Laurent Jalabert to take the lead.

"He made it so easy that it was beautiful," said Jalabert. "I am honored I was the last one that he passed."

A few days later, Armstrong rode into Paris, winner of his third Tour de France in a row. Almost immediately, everyone began talking about what he would do in 2002.

But 2001 had one more victory for Lance — a victory over cancer. On October 18, he was told that he was cancer-free. His own fight against the disease had been a success, but he knew the worldwide battle against cancer was far from over. When not racing or training, Armstrong devoted time and energy to the Lance Armstrong Foundation, dedicated to helping others deal with their own fight with cancer.

By 2002, Lance Armstrong was one of the most recognized athletes in the world. His courageous struggle against cancer plus his victories in the Tour de France had made him a hero and ensured that all eyes would be on him whenever he raced. He did not disappoint. In the first half of the year, he placed in the top four of seven races. Then, on July 6, the Tour de France began.

Armstrong started out with a win in the prologue, but the yellow jersey passed to another racer, Rubens Bertogliati, in the first stage. Over the next eight stages, Lance bounced from third place down to eighth, and then up to second. He was still in second when the race course headed into the Pyrenees Mountains.

The mountain stages of the Tour are so difficult that they often slow or even stop the best bikers. But not Lance Armstrong. With the help and protection of his USPS teammates, he won the eleventh and twelfth stages. His overall time at this point was nearly two and a half minutes better than the second place rider. By the end of the fourteenth stage, his lead had grown to more than four minutes. But it wasn't until the second to last stage — when he beat second place rider Joseba Beloki of Spain by two minutes, eleven seconds — that his victory was assured once and for all.

Lance rode into Paris wearing the coveted Maillot Jaune for the fourth year in a row. With a total race time of eighty-two hours, five minutes, and twelve seconds; he finished seven minutes, seventeen seconds ahead of Beloki. His average speed for the race was 39.88 kilometers per hour.

Armstrong knew that his USPS teammates deserved much of the credit for his victory. "The first (win) was the comeback, the second one confirmation, the third a really good time, and this year was the year of the team," he said. "Cycling is a team sport. You need protection in the flats, and in the mountains. That security blanket makes a big difference. Some people talked about this team being the best in the history of cycling . . . Give me these nine guys on the start line next year."

The 90th Tour de France was scheduled to kick off in Paris on July 5, 2003. Speculation was high that Lance Armstrong would soon join the handful of riders who had won five Tours. Unfortunately, at the start of the race, the defending champion was suffering from a stomach ailment and tendonitis in his hips. He placed a disappointing seventh in the prologue.

In fact, difficulties seemed to plague Armstrong and other bikers for much of the Tour. Five hundred meters before the end of the first stage, he and thirty cyclists crashed in a devastating pileup that left one rider with a cracked collarbone and two others hospitalized and out of the race for good. Armstrong managed to finish the stage despite a badly bruised thigh.

Meanwhile, temperatures on the course soared

to more than one hundred degrees. Armstrong became seriously dehydrated at one stage, something he later said was a "near fatal mistake." He recovered, only to narrowly escape another collision a few days later when archrival Joseba Beloki lost control and crashed right in front of him. Armstrong veered clear of Beloki, rode across a field, and rejoined his team. Beloki, on the other hand, suffered a broken elbow, femur, and finger and had to abandon the race.

More trouble came in the fifteenth stage of the race, when a spectator clipped Armstrong's right handlebar, jerking Armstrong and his bike off balance. Armstrong tumbled head over heels but, amazingly, managed to regain his bike and finish the stage — in first place!

The remainder of the Tour was uneventful for Armstrong, and as he had done the previous four years, he coasted into Paris wearing the Maillot Jaune. He had won only two stages and at eighty-three hours, forty-one minutes, and twelve seconds his race time was slower than in 2002 — not surprising after the difficulties he'd faced throughout the three-week race. But none of that seemed to matter to Armstrong as he took the podium at the Champs-Elysées. With the victory, he became the fifth cyclist to win the Tour de France five times.

Now the question was, would he, and could he, go for a record-breaking consecutive sixth win in 2004?

Chapter Thirteen:
2004

The Ride of His Life

After the 2003 Tour, Lance Armstrong took some time off from cycling to support the Tour of Hope, a weeklong ride to raise money for the Lance Armstrong Foundation. He also spent time promoting his book, *Every Second Counts*, and the foundation. When asked about his plans for 2004 and the Tour de France, he made his position perfectly clear: "I'll be back next year to win. I'm not looking for second place!"

Armstrong knew that another win would depend not only on his own ability but on the support he received from his eight teammates. Six of those riders had been members of USPS the previous year, while two were newcomers. Some were strong mountain riders capable of giving Lance the protection he needed on steep inclines and sharp descents, while others worked best on the flatlands and straightaways.

"We have a very experienced team and more than anything else, we have a very committed team," Lance said of the USPS squad. "They know what it takes to win the Tour and they want to do that again."

The Tour began on July 3, a blustery day that ended with Armstrong coming in two seconds behind lead rider Fabian Cancellara of Switzerland. The next day was even windier, with a drizzling rain that left the roads dangerously slick. Lance dropped to third place; by the end of the third stage, he had fallen to fourth.

In past Tours, Armstrong was always at his strongest when climbing and descending through the mountains, and this year would prove to be no different. As the course wound through the Pyrenees, he fought the top rivals for the choicest positions in the turns. He forced his legs and lungs to power him up and over the steepest hills and pushed himself to maintain top speed and complete control on the declines. With each stage, the difference between his overall time and that of the leader grew less and less. By the end of Phase II, Lance was only twenty-two seconds behind the first place cyclist, twenty-five-year-old Thomas Voeckler of France.

Voeckler had been a professional rider for only four seasons and was a virtual unknown in the cycling world. But in the 2004 Tour de France, he became France's darling by earning and hanging on to the Maillot Jaune from the fifth through the fourteenth stages, the best effort seen by a French-born rider in years. But the race wasn't over yet.

Throughout Phase II, Armstrong had slowly been gaining on the young Voeckler. At the end of stage eleven, he was nine minutes, thirty-five seconds behind. By the end of stage twelve, he had narrowed the margin by more than four minutes. Lance earned his second stage win of the Tour the next day — and closed the gap to a mere twenty-two seconds behind Voeckler.

Voeckler managed to hang on to his lead through the fourteenth stage, the last of Phase II. He had worn the yellow jersey for ten days. He would not wear it an eleventh day. In fact, at the close of the fifteenth stage, Voeckler would be in eighth place, almost nine and a half minutes behind the new Tour leader — Lance Armstrong.

Thanks in large part to the tremendous cooperative effort of the USPS team, Armstrong edged out not just Voeckler, but all other top contenders (including Jan Ullrich and Andreas Kloden, both on the T-Mobile team from Germany, and Italian Ivan Basso of Team CSC). He was nearly a minute and a half in front of second place Basso going into the sixteenth stage.

Stage sixteen was an individual time trial, a test of speed, control, and endurance as riders covered fifteen and a half kilometers through twenty-one switchbacks up a steep grade. It was a difficult ride under normal circumstances. But as it turned out, the circumstances were far from normal for Lance.

Spectators from several countries lined the course. Many were disappointed that Lance had outridden their favorite cyclists. They decided that Lance didn't deserve their applause so instead, as he rode past them, they taunted him, spat on him, cursed him, and even scrawled angry messages to him on the pavement. Such appalling treatment might have broken the spirit of another man, but not Lance. He did his best to ignore it, hoping that his actions would speak louder than their words.

In the end, they did. Four days and four grueling stages later, Lance Armstrong rode into Paris and climbed the steps to the podium of the Champs-Elysées for the sixth year in a row. He had completed the 3395 kilometer race in eighty-three hours, thirty-six minutes, and two seconds, covering an average of 40.56 kilometers an hour.

As the music of "The Star-Spangled Banner" played, he had this to say about his record-breaking victory: "It hasn't sunk in yet. But six, standing on the top step on the podium on the Champs-Elysées, is really special. The Tour de France is the most beautiful race in the world . . . It's as if I was with my five friends and we were 13 years old and we all had new bikes and we said, 'Okay, we're going to race from here to there.' You want to beat your friends more than anything. You're sprinting and you're attacking. It was like that for me. A simple pleasure."

Only time will tell if Lance Armstrong will pursue that "simple pleasure" in 2005. He certainly has enough to keep him busy if he chooses not to. In 2004, the Lance Armstrong Foundation and Nike launched a new fundraising campaign called Wear Yellow Live Strong. For one dollar, supporters can purchase a simple yellow rubber wristband engraved with the words *Live Strong*. All funds collected will help support the Lance Armstrong Foundation's goal of teaching people about cancer and cancer survivorship.

But if Armstrong does decide to enter the Tour de France in 2005, he won't be there for the scenery. "If I'm here," he said at the end of the 2004 competition, "I race to win."

Matt Christopher®

Sports Bio Bookshelf

Lance Armstrong

Kobe Bryant

Jennifer Capriati

Julie Foudy

Jeff Gordon

Wayne Gretzky

Ken Griffey Jr.

Mia Hamm

Tony Hawk

Grant Hill

Ichiro

Derek Jeter

Randy Johnson

Michael Jordan

Mario Lemieux

Tara Lipinski

Mark McGwire

Greg Maddux

Hakeem Olajuwon

Shaquille O'Neal

Alex Rodriguez

Curt Schilling

Briana Scurry

Sammy Sosa

Venus and
Serena Williams

Tiger Woods

Steve Young

The #1
Sports Series
for Kids

Read them all!

*Originally published as *Crackerjack Halfback*

All available in paperback from Little, Brown and Company